Arctic

Coral Reef

WORLD WILDLIFE FUND

Hab

ISBN 0-7683-2045-3

Published in 1998 by Cedco Publishing Company,
100 Pelican Way, San Rafael, CA 94901.
Produced by Jennifer Barry Design, Sausalito, CA.
Text by Blake Hallanan.

For a free catalog of our entire line of books, write us at the address above,
visit our website: www.cedco.com or e-mail us at: sales@cedco.com

The Panda Device and WWF are registered trademarks.
Printed in Hong Kong.

itats

A Sticker Activity Book

Savannah

AFRICA

Savannahs are flat grasslands with wet and dry seasons where lots of different kinds of animals live. In order to survive, some of them graze the grasslands and others feed on the trees and shrubs that grow in abundance. The big, predatory animals feed on the grazers. The open plains of a savannah allow animals to move to a new place when they need fresh grass, water, or mud holes to wallow in. Africa has large savannahs but there are many other savannahs found on different continents.

Lion

- I need to eat up to 15 pounds of meat a day—mostly antelope, gazelle, warthog, and zebra.
- I live in a family called a pride that includes from 4 to 12 adult females and 1 to 6 adult males.
- I need plenty of space to hunt, so the open savannah is ideal for me. I hunt mostly at night while the other animals are resting.

Giraffe

- I eat from trees called thorn acacias that are found mainly on the savannah.
- I have a very powerful kick and can harm an attacking lion.
- I am the tallest of all land creatures and can reach trees and plants that are out of reach for other animals.

Impala

- I need to drink water twice a day, so I live near water holes on the savannah.
- I can run up to 60 miles per hour to escape the lions, cheetahs, leopards, and spotted hyenas who hunt me.
- I stay near groups of antelope for better protection from lions and other predators.

Zebra

- I travel with my family and other zebras in a herd. Our black and white stripes create confusion for our enemies, making it difficult for them to single one of us out.
- If I see an enemy, I make short, loud snorts to warn the other zebras in my herd.
- We move across the plains of the African savannah in large groups, grazing on fresh, green grass.
- I also like to eat grass-like plants called sedges that grow in the savannah.

Cheetah

- I can sprint faster than any other animal—up to 70 miles per hour.
- I tend to hunt in the middle of the day when other hunters are sleeping.
- I eat impalas, gazelles, hares, jackals, and young warthogs. I sometimes wait in the branches of a low tree until they get very close and then I take them by surprise.
- When I can't find enough water I eat juicy melons some-times found in the savannah.

Black Rhinoceros

- I have a long, pointed upper lip that helps me browse for my food—mostly leaves and the ends of shrubs.
- I'm one of the biggest animals found on the African savannah and I can weigh up to 3,000 pounds.
- If an enemy attacks me, I may charge at them and use my horn for protection.
- I prefer to live by myself.

Hyena

- I am a very good hunter, but I'm also good at finding food that other animals have left behind.
- I often hide my extra food in muddy pools found in the African savannah, and I return to my hiding place when I'm hungry again.
- I can make up to 17 sounds, including loud screams of anger when I'm trying to scare off lions.
- I can spend up to 10 hours a day hunting and often cover more than 20 miles.

Hippo-potamus

- I live mostly in slow-moving rivers and lakes of the African savannah.
- My eyes, ears, and nose are on top of my head so I can see, hear, and breathe air while I'm almost completely under water.
- I come out of the water at night to graze for about 6 hours, mostly on patches of grass.

Ostrich

- I am the world's largest living bird and can be 8 feet tall and weigh 300 pounds.
- I have poorly devel-oped flight muscles, so instead of flying, I run fast across the plains of the savannah at up to 30 miles per hour.
- I eat leaves, flowers, seeds, and sometimes lizards and tortoises.

African Elephant

- I eat up to 300 pounds of grass, leaves, twigs, and other plant food every day.
- I bathe in mud and dust to protect myself from the hot sun and insects.
- I need to drink water every day and I can hold more than 2 gallons in my trunk.

Tropical Rain Forest

SOUTH
AMERICA

There are tropical rain forests all over the world and though they have much in common, each of them has many different types of animals and plants. What the tropical rain forests have in common is heat, rain, and very tall trees which collect as much sunlight as possible to feed the forest. Most small animals can stay safely hidden in the treetops eating leaves, fruits and insects. Because of the abundance of moisture in the trees, these animals don't have to risk finding water on the ground. With an abundance of solar energy, tropical rain forests grow many sweet-smelling flowers and unusual fruits. The largest tropical rain forests are in South America, Asia, Africa, and Madagascar.

Jaguar

- I swim and climb well but stalk my prey on the ground.
- I eat deer, monkeys, birds, turtles, frogs, and fish.
- I live in the dense forest of swamps with good cover and easy access to water.
- I often bury my food so I can eat it later.
- I have spotted fur like the leopard and cheetah, my African cousins.

Blue Morpho Butterfly

- I spend my days circling around the tops of jungle trees in the rain forest.
- I rarely descend to Earth but can occasionally be seen on the ground drinking from puddles or licking fallen fruit.
- I am shiny and brightly colored because of the way the scales of my wings reflect the light.
- I have a wing span of up to 7 inches.

Spider Monkey

- I am called a spider monkey because of my long legs and tail.
- I like to stay in the tops of trees eating fruit and leaf shoots.
- I can travel many miles in a single day with a small group of other spider monkeys looking for food.
- I am the largest monkey in South and Central America.
- I weigh about 30 pounds and can measure about five feet from head to tail.

Rainbow Boa Constrictor

- I'm called a constrictor because I kill birds, lizards, and small rodents by squeezing them to death and swallowing them whole.
- I hunt animals by hanging from trees and looking like a big vine.
- I can live for long periods of time without eating because I digest my food slowly.
- I defend myself by striking and biting, but I am not poisonous.

Tamarin

- I live in a family group with about five other tamarins.
- I live high in the trees and sleep at night in tree cavities.
- I eat mostly fruit and nectar and I also search out insects under bark and leaves.
- Most of us are born with a twin brother or sister.

Macaw

- I am the largest of the rain forest parrots and have the most brightly colored feathers.
- I have a strong, hooked beak that has scissor-like cutting edges which are so strong that I can split open tough shells of Brazil nuts.
- I often use one of my feet to hold food up to my mouth.

Red-Eyed Tree Frog

- My bright red eyes are my most distinguishing feature.
- I have large suction-like toe pads to help me cling to branches and leaves where I live.
- I am mostly active at night.
- I spend my days resting on plant leaves.

Toucan

- I spend most of my life high in the tree tops eating, breeding, and bathing in the rain water.
- I am a fruit-eater and I often toss a piece up in the air into my mouth.
- My long, colorful bill is very light-weight and allows me to stretch out to pick fruit from other branches.

Coatimundi

- I am very good at climbing trees.
- I eat turtle and crocodile eggs but I also eat frogs, fruits, and small rodents and I use my long snout to grub for insects.
- I live up to 14 years.
- My enemies are large cats, boa constrictors, and large birds.

Tapir

- I eat mostly grass, leaves, buds, twigs, and fruits.
- I'm a very good swimmer and spend much time in the water feeding, cooling off and getting rid of skin parasites.
- I'm also a good climber and can scramble up river banks and steep mountain sides.
- My main enemy is the jaguar.

Arctic

ARCTIC

The polar lands are the coldest places in the world and for much of the year the ground is frozen. The Arctic is so cold because of the way the Earth moves around the sun. The sun's rays are not very strong at the poles. Few animals can live here all year round because most of the land is covered in snow or ice. The winters are dark with just a little daylight and in the summer the sky is bright all day and night. During the summer, the snow and ice begin to melt.

Walrus

- I have flippers instead of legs.
- I dig with my snout to find clams, mussels and other sea creatures to eat.
- I use my tusks like ice axes to help break holes in the ice.
- I have plenty of fat to keep me warm.
- I can live up to 40 years.

Arctic Hare

- I'm very good at digging burows and tunnels where I go to stay protected.
- My white fur disguises me very well in winter.
- When the snow melts I grow a gray-brown coat of fur.

Atlantic Puffin

- I'm sometimes called a sea parrot because of my colorful head feathers.
- I can hold up to 28 fish in my beak.
- I leave my cliff-top burrow in the winter and head out to sea where it's warmer.
- I weigh about one pound and can live for 25-30 years.

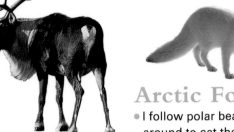

Reindeer

- I have wide hooves that make it easier for me to walk in deep snow and to scrape snow away to eat lichens and mosses.
- Sometimes in winter I migrate to a pine forest if it gets too cold.
- I have distinctive tree-shaped antlers on my head, whether I'm a male or female.

Arctic Fox

- I follow polar bears around to eat the scraps of food they leave behind.
- I only start to shiver when it gets to be 70 degrees below zero.
- I usually live in a group with one male and several females called vixens.
- I have fur covering the soles of my feet to keep me warm.

Harp Seal

- I am an underwater hunter and eat mostly fish, shrimp, and squid.
- I have a thick layer of fat called blubber which helps me to stay warm.
- I can swim to 2,000 feet below the surface.
- I can close my nostrils and hold my breath for more than an hour.

Snowy Owl

- I hunt during the long arctic days of summer.
- I have yellow eyes and my toes and legs are covered with white feathers.
- I breed only when there are enough mice available to feed my babies.
- I also eat voles, lemmings, and other small animals including alpine hares.

Gray Wolf

- I eat deer, moose, and reindeer.
- Following the migration of my prey, I travel with a small pack of other wolves looking for food.
- I sleep a lot in the winter to save energy.

Arctic Tern

- I have the longest migration of any animal and will fly 25,000 miles in a year from the Arctic to the Antarctic and back.
- I swallow fish whole right after I catch them.
- I breed in the tundra during the short arctic summer.

Polar Bear

- I have very thick fur to keep me warm.
- I am the largest living four-legged, meat-eating animal, and I feed on seals, small whales, and walruses.
- I'm a very good swimmer and can stay in ice-cold water for hours.
- I have five long, curved claws to help me grip the slippery ice.

Coral Reef

AUSTRALIA

Corals are small animals that grow close together. Many protect themselves by building hard cases. As the coral animals grow up and die, their skeletons pile up and in some places form big banks called coral reefs. Coral can only grow in warm, shallow water where there is plenty of sunlight.

The Great Barrier Reef is the world's largest coral reef. It stretches more than 1,240 miles off the northeastern coast of Australia and is actually 210 separate reefs. Coral reefs are efficient habitats because every available source of food is used and recycled by the plants and animals that live there.

Sea Turtle

- Although I breathe air, I spend my life at sea and can hold my breath for hours at a time.
- I go on land only to lay my eggs in the sand and then leave them to hatch.
- I can live for more than 100 years and weigh up to 1,300 pounds.
- I eat a variety of food including seaweed, jellyfish, crabs, and fish.
- When I'm diving deep, I can slow my heartbeat to conserve oxygen.

Clownfish

- My bright colors make it difficult for me to hide from my enemies.
- I stay close to the tentacles of an animal called a sea anemone whose stinging tentacles hurt my enemies but not me.
- I eat plankton and sea plants.

Sea Anemone

- I look like a plant but I'm a sea animal with long, stinging tentacles which I use to trap small creatures like shrimp and small fish as they float by.
- My tentacles pass my food down to my mouth opening, and spread out again to catch more fish.
- The clownfish lives within my tentacles and we help protect and feed each other.

Sea Star

- Most of us have five arms.
- I have suckers on the bottoms of each of my five arms that I use to move and cling to coral.
- I feed myself through my mouth which is in the middle of my underside.
- I eat shellfish and coral and help the reef from growing too large.

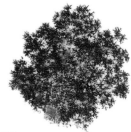

Gorgonian Coral

- I have soft, flexible, branches that are shaped like a bush or a tree.
- I am made of colorful, horny material.
- My name means "coral" in Latin.

Lionfish

- My bright colors act as a warning to other fish to stay away.
- Hidden behind my dorsal fin are spines that can inject a deadly poison into my attacker.
- I swim in shallow waters around the reefs and rocks.

Sea Horse

- I swim upright drifting in the sea.
- I grow up in a pouch in my daddy's tummy.
- When I'm young I can eat as many as 3,500 tiny shrimp in a day.
- My jaws are hollow like a drinking straw.
- When I rest I coil my tail around sea plants.
- I'm called a sea horse because my head is shaped like that of a horse.

Staghorn Coral

- I have hard branches that are shaped like the antlers of a male deer.
- I can grow a new branch in the reef from just a tiny broken piece of myself.
- My branches grow upward toward the sunlight.

Hermit Crab

- I take my home (usually an empty snail shell) with me wherever I go.
- I use my mouth to sift through sand looking for food and I use my pincers to catch shellfish and other food.
- When I grow too big for one shell I move to a larger one.
- I hide in rock pools and burrow in the sand.

Angelfish

- I swim in a group called a school. Our stripes protect us by creating a colorful pattern that confuses our enemies.
- I have strong teeth to pull pieces of sponge, coral, and plants called algae from the reef for my food.
- I hover near small caves in the coral reef so I can swim inside quickly if I sense danger.
- My flat body allows me to slip easily through narrow gaps in the coral.